Where Poetry Dwells

Connie Holt

BOOKSIDE Press

BookSide Press
877-741-8091
www.booksidepress.com
orders@booksidepress.com

Contents

Girls in a Picture

Light Free Nature flowers
A peaceful sense of well-being
As the water ebbs and flows
By a quiet creek
Sunlight slips away peacefully
And meek
You can almost feel the breeze
So warm and sweet
Water lapped on gray rocks
Ducks swim near the dock
A girl any minute going to
Lift her fan and use it.
Old and very rustic
You can almost feel how warm
It is
The way she's got her head back
And yes, she's too warm
Any minute she's going to fan
Her face and neck.

Life

Life is an ember…
The glowing remains of life
Through pain and grief and strife
Breath is its keeper
A guardian of the soul
That heal in sleep
The heart is a boundary
The gate that will swing wide
And welcome you inside
Life to share is all there is
It need not all ways be the
Best to shine
Even in the worst times
A door with no bay
A mist through which you
Could not see.

Timeless Teardrops

Tears hide in corners
Gusts of impulse, I cannot control
My heart cries forgiveness
As my mind lets go
It's hard to see through
Our swollen tears
To fight the passing years
Along they sked silent tears
Life-giving words are hard
To write
And true devotion to hold
On tight
They said, Christmas won't
Be the same this year
Because you won't be here
But I know better than that
You'll be here in my heart
Till you come back
While you serve to keep our
Country free
It helps me realize God's place for me.

The Miracle of Christmas

Today is the only day on your calendar
God's one eternal worth,
Hearts gather in the wonder
Of Jesus's birth
We share that feeling of joy
The arrival of Christmas in our hearts.
Christmas is a glowing light
That sets our lives apart
Christmas is a starry night
Of joyous angels' songs
Christmas is a manger
Illuminated by stars above
God's miracle of peace and
Hope and love

Growing Up

Her resolutions and decisions were forgotten
Its contents left in a box
They weren't important at this time
She has a specified position on line
A down payment on becoming
A grown woman
What important knowing full
What she's doing any giving moment
She began to grow up
To fill her cup
Then she began to learn a new concern
As if the girl who had gone up
The hill was a different one,
Who had come down it.
Like Pandora's tempting box,
Curious to turn the key, that
Locks new ways to yearn.

Angel's Wings

On angel's wings you were taken.
But in my heart you will stay
All through winter and into spring
For golden sunrises in the sky
Sunsets that kiss each day goodbye
Lights like colorful jewels
Rain and snow
Middle of heaven stands a rainbow
Know the joy of perfect rest
We know we have been blessed
On angel's wings you lifted up,
And taken to the mountaintop
To heaven up above
Protected by God's love
Now day has begun
Dawn awaits the sun
Glorious breaks the rosy light
That shines forever bright.

When Soldiers Don't Come Home

Lightning brightly vein the darkening sky
Ferocious storm of midday night
Fleeing birds, their screeching rise
Across a fading sun
Leave tracks speak to silence, yet
Remark upon this day
Find their memories haunts the spaces in our mind
Sorrow winter chills here on earth
Once fertile our heart
Now lies barren for the largest part
On cold, hardened ground we weep alone
When soldiers don't come home
Memories fade quickly weaker
Carried off out of reach
Our breath continue their painful song
Soothing sounds of silence, as we heard an echo.

I'm Coming Home

Walk as time stands so still
By the flowing stream
The stream ceases to flow as
Time stands ever so still
When I touch the hem of
Autumn's dress
I'll be home
Walk under quilted jewels
Where baby stars dwell
Unborn clouds to porch upon
My soul
Captured a patch of heaven
In my hands
Sing with the angels' band
God keep my soul
In his heavenly city beyond
The brightest clear sky
Hold on to his hand, let him
Lead the way
I cross the flowing stream
Dwells God's abiding love
In the heavenly realm
Of heaven's golden light
Here my Jordan flows

King David

God is watching over the story of our lives
As the case of King David
Just a boy standing with his sheep
The Lord was in his keep
David slew the massive giant called Goliath
Who fell under God's wrath
Here I stepped into my notes
That was something worth to know
God is watching over the story of our lives
Help us to overcome obstacles we face in life
As we learned
As a shepherd boy, David tended his father's sheep
For he was ordered in God's steps
He learned lessons of God's love
Angels sent from God above
Later wrote the beautiful shepherd psalms
On the twenty-third song

We Have This Moment

Hold tight to the sound of the music
Before it suddenly disappears
Into the sunset of the years
Time has an end of days
Make memories what is today
To touch before it slips away
Have this moment to hold in our hands
To review memories we have made
Remember—the years are fleeting may be today
Might be the last one you see
Released gentle moments each float free

Lord's Supper Table

Come to the supper table with the Lord from on high
Where: in the heavenly realm in the sky
Jesus is here his door is open
He is at the head of the table, waiting for you
Hands outstretched waiting for his child anew
The table is set all you need
Wisdom, love, understanding knowledge indeed
Plenty to talk and facts to know
A child of his will surely show
Love blanketed him
The glorious tone of the Lord
Telling us to "come on in."

Perfect on Paper

My heart sputtered with a few extra beats
My heart full of the spirit next time we meet
I considered penning a letter to carry into another week
The thought distracted me enough to seek
Upon my heart as words, lies before me
Perfect on paper and free
A thought did stir
Gliding on paper
In my heart, I write of you
In my heart, I write of me

A Tear-Stained Heart

Nothing speaks to the soul like our despair
Leaving one to question?
No one is ever truly prepared
A tear so small carries so much emotions
Grievance become our portion
She was our sunflowers
Those sunflowers still speak
Giving us what we need
To keep her memory
But in the time she was here, lives were touched
Memories were made and bonds
Were formed to last forever

Forever in My Heart

A precious bond pressing on the corner of my mind
Eternal ties I couldn't leave behind
No photos of a life on this earth do we have to show
No memories of a smile or a first step to share
No sound of a first word or laughter did we hear
My mind couldn't remain there long
The depth and maturity of both heart and spirit
Just become too strong
One day, we'll see your sweet face and hear your voice
We'll hold you close
Throughout all eternity in our heavenly home.

Pearl Morning

The frosty winds carried a spray of sleet
The crystal patterns of ice underneath my feet
Frosty snowflakes blow in white against the soft air
And beauty everywhere…
Glittering jewels beyond the spread of a pearl morning
Silvery glowing lights to add beauty to adorn
In sweet colors
An icicle frosty white
A painter light
Reflected beneath an icicle frosty blue
Anything clear bluer

Orange-Ginger

Sunburst skies—
Sugar and spice—
Curtained white sugar clouds
A ray here, a ray there as the color-mistaken
Orange-ginger to be awaken
Touch my thoughts
A painter of light soft as tears
A poet's every verse
Where safe the ancient pages keep where the dreams
Never let their special light dim
The dance and the poems sleep, sacred to keep
The whispered winds speak softly of their secret
Who lies here fast asleep

Secondhand Heart

God's world is decorated so artistically
God is the master artist
The heart is made from scraps and secondhand
Never the original the whole piece
From making something beautiful God gives us
The ability to do that with that piece
How much of a gift does
He give us
To patch scraps together of our lives
To bring him glory?
Simple leftovers better than itself
I don't have much of a heart to give
It's scraps—a secondhand
The Lord could accomplish
Much with time

Patch of Heaven

Sometimes a rose grows in winter
We miss it for the snow
Winter jewels—blue like sea crystals
Winter—cold ignored the
Curious feeling of anger at coldness
Ignored loving kindness
The rose's loving hand gave birth to days
Patch of heaven
Relegated the coldness even
A tiny amount of light shining down
Tiptoeing up on a fall morning frost all around
Winter left here…
The frigid air stayed near.

Twelve Steps in Christmas

I feel the crisp cool all around
And whiteness covers all the ground
Cold winter shackled us indoors
Nest to the woodstove
To living warmth in the circle of God's above
At Christmas a list of gifts is from Jesus
Who loves us:
The twelve steps in Christmas
With God's signature
The true treasure:
An old story told
The blessed savior's birth, I'd
Love to unfold
God sent his gift of love for all
One of eternal worth;
Jesus came to earth.

In His Gentle Ways

Jesus held me when I cry
And see the world through tears
Warmed with an inner peace
That drives away my fears
My steps are ordered by God
In his gentle ways
I trust in him day-to-day
God does not give me what
I can handle
He leads me by his candle
God help me to handle
What I was given
He taught me how to
Have eternal life
A testimonial to his love
Left here behind to put in place
God's the light that will not fail
God blessed me with his grace

In a Narrow View

Words I cannot say stir up
All the emptiness of me
Worldliness words smalls barely
Enough I see
Each day will be different
In a narrow view
A new challenge be few
Take one day at a time
Take that last climb
You will be amazed
You'll be given a prize
God stepped in time changed
Our dimensions
Wrote us into a new future
Important and pure
Every day is about Jesus
He is always with us
For all I have and all I see
Dearest Lord, I owe to thee!

Master January

January is never still
Controls a cold air of a strong will
Rules the yearly seasons without a reason
Winter creeps in—a blanket of snow
A time for all things to rest
The yawning clouds that stretch the sky
Little bit of sunlight had a chance to hang on
To aspire beyond the means to liquify
Fierce cold exposed their toes
In a steady harsh flow
Many a day comes a chill
To complete amount fulfill.

The Past—The Present

Today to an old home place
Where I used to play
No familiar voice called, "Come in,"
Nor as I left "Come back again."
For only the chimney stood straight and tall
In the distance a lonely love call
A spring once flowed cold and sweet
Filled leaves at my feet
I closed my eyes and could see it
As it was back when
I saw myself a little girl
Some things can't settle in my mind
Like past or present
They haunt my sleep
Stop nor keep

Song in the Dark

Song in the dark
Night of all nights
Oh holy night
Angels descending stars
Shining bright
A savior has come from
Heaven above
God sent his son, a sign
Of his love
Song in the dark
Angels with an announcement
Loud and clear
God's blessings so dear
Of joyous angels' songs
From yonder ransomed throng
From whom all blessings flow
That night of long ago
Song in the dark
The blessed savior's birth
Is a landmark

Boots

He wears spurs on his boots
And a ten-gallon hat,
And he feels at home in an
Old pair of jeans
He is lost in the world of
Make-believe
And delight with the echoes
That resound
With cool breezes blowing
All around
The two of us it always seems
Are always making up stories
And splendid dreams
When we were small it was such
A pleasure to be together
Times have changed and have we
Yet and in our eyes its children we all see
It's so real, something not everyone can feel
Brother and sister who have we overcome
The blisters of life and made it such
A divine and peaceful flight

Easter

From Jesus's birth
To his resurrection
God redeemed us in the
Resurrection of Jesus
Easter:
Love Jesus has for us
God cares for us each
Through dark days filled
With answers
His love, the love
Promise of his eternal worth
Our redeemer's birth
The glorious morning
The ascension day
The glorious news
End of the sabbath first of the
Week, come Mary Magdalen to,
See the sepulcher where Jesus lay
Seeing an angel was told he risen
And go tell his disciples
This same Jesus is coming again, as
The brighter sunrise

The Sun Caught Me Smiling

Autumn leaves are dancing for me.
I hear the birds sing in the trees
Violet raindrops, red ribbons in the sky
The sun caught me smiling
Blue orchids, jeweled coaches in meadows of icicles
Silvered streams and golden sunshine are riches
A gift of sight the sun caught me smiling
That I might see whence come the light
Flames melting like candies, wax figures meant to be
Let this life fulfill and see.

Little Blue Truck (for Renee)

Life-giving words are letters to me
It seems like only yesterday
That you were crawling
Across the floor,
Honey. When now you want
To drive a little blue truck
I worry until you are in the house
I cannot sleep till then
I'll always be a grandmother
And you'll understand it when
You'll be a mother someday
And I will watch it all
My grandchildren come to play
And pick them up when they fall

Autumn Glaze

We step into this story like
A blanket pulled over the sky
Unfurling slowly but the time seems to fly
The gentle gray light of morning
Found me still asleep
Regular times play hide-and-seek
There were black clouds but the sun wears the crown
Colorful jewels, their multicolored
Lights of the autumn glaze
Put it all in a new phase
But the sky it weeps bit of frost
Until autumn is lost
Wind have more bite
Day melds more quickly to night
The autumn glaze—
Bring us light of praise

Calendar Girl

For arranging time into days
I gradually understood what I had to say
By fireside and candlelight I
Came to know the poetry in her soul
And while the heart has its
Seasons, hers wore the face of love
To leave to the velvet dark of bright
Silk and satin dreams
A soul is a dream to catch a glimpse of her
A beautiful light shining down on
A secret garden of her soul
One cannot grow old
One greater than all the beauty I see
All the love is laced to me.

Puppy Love

Ears are smitten with melodies
One perfect song their hearts can sing
Their hearts serenade the approach of their love
Surely the whole world must know
These things from above
Young at heart wrap in their magic
Glow of puppy love
So filled with promise
Dropping moonbeams from the sky
A silver song way up high
All they hold dear
One of love so near
A thought still time to say
Wait for each new day
Young hearts wondered in thought of
Life if they will find
In everyday life being loving and kind.

Fairy

One of crystal clear
One as love so near
Eyes full of jewels all wrapped
In her magic glow
One is of the midnight sun
One wake at dawn with glee
To face another with thee
I am there in time to capture
The moment of reality
She has dreamt and concealed
The impossibilities
As the fairy's song
And dreams wait in her sleep and peers
'Round the corners and watch
From a high place with the sun
(-) the hilltops one by one
In the last vestiges of fading light
Then usher in a waiting night

A Little Dove

She soared through the sky with privacy
And plucked us from our grieving hearts
In the listening stillness was the best part
A song into my bed at night
I heard a flutter in the breeze
I saw a shadow in the trees
When all is still at night
I hear tiny wings in flight
So wherever you go I know it's true
I'll hear you from that perfect tree it's you
Let your spirit more soar, to sing unending song
Melody sweet and strong
Beliefs of a folklore

The Circle

Could I find a jewel so rare
As my granddaughter's heart?
Could precious gems give the
Radiance her smile imparts?
A rose's white petals are the
Richness of her heart
The leaves so green are the
Richness of her soul
The thorns the heartaches
We have to endure
The stem the ladder we climb, to
Reach the petals
The circle a point in a line to the center
We are circled to our hearts
Inviting love to enter

At Grandma's

When it comes to Grandma,
I only look inside my heart
Love dwells within that
Cannot break apart
The purity of her character
Makes a perfect day
She touched so many lives on
Her life's pathway
This was Grandma
One favorite time at Grandma's
Watching her bake bread
Another time, sleeping in her big
Feather bed
The light goes off
I cross my heart
I pray to kiss Grandma in the morn
I pray to see her once more

Old and Forgotten

A thought in memory never forgotten
Soon comes a lot
It's hard to believe how much
My life has changed
What along the path will lead
This is a remainder to hold on
And reflect upon
I bought my thoughts back
To the present
I didn't have time to daydream but I
Knew what that meant
I'm old and forgotten
At the end fade quickly carried
Off out reach
Sad my thoughts as the river
Runs onto a beach
Forced a day gone where all must go
In the light of an afterglow

The Rose Garden

The loving hand of God has given birth today
A beautiful light shining down
On a secret garden
Transformed happiness in unexpected ways
A testimonial of his love
To whisper words of hope and peace from above
A ruby cardinal rehearses his rendition of a popular song
Hold me in the promise of morning
When night is long
The sky reflects a (-) comparable to a sapphire jewel
That cast a shine renewal
Clouds like soft cotton balls swinging in the sky
The Lord's mercies lead the way.

Time Won't Let Me

You stop the hand of God you
Rob the giver of a blessing
Raindrops dancing in puddles
Calms the cause of distress
Life changes in ways you never saw coming
True worth is in good
Not in dreaming time won't let me
While there is time, I need to see
To the things
Joy to hearts in trials it can comfort bring
As love it does import
Time won't let me afford to neglect
The good things to collect
To gather in one place
The blessings of each day
Of God's grace

In My Bible

The poems I had written and softly read,
In my Bible
Seemed to fill my poetic needs
Has a purpose to succeed
A card saying, "Hi, Grandma!"
You should have a mother's day
That's fun and happy too
In my soul, I call it happiness
To be loved with so much tenderness
In my Bible
Tucked inside my heart's pocket
Worn like a locket
A really special grandma
And you guessed it!
That means you!
In my Bible, between the pages,
Lays my card too.

Before Flowers Are Given

Flowers given or spoken, hear
Their words of kindness
Give pause for enduring tenderness
Flowers don't betray what found in the heart
The presence of love celebrates that
Must wait sets their lives apart
That you could hear and give you a tear
They've made the way quite clear
But rain must fall before flowers are given
For their care to thrive
The rain softness made not a sound
Confronting us with strong power
Gently flooding down
Pure and precious start
Tender loving care keeping their part

The Notebook

Beginning:
Love is reported to my heart from her,
Mom and child we were
A mother is a gardener of God
Tending to hearts of her children
Abiding love I know to the end
When God sprinkled stars in the heaven he saved
A few for the gleam in her eyes
He took some warmth from the sun
For her warm, loving smile
Her spirit seemed to fit together,
To make one perfect person
God chose her to be the one
In the notebook
A small admiring word
I put into writing
She loved me as only she could.

Christmas Card

Sparse cottony clouds,
In laced sky snowflakes
Dressing silvery string, of
Ribbons—an ice lake
Freezing temperatures
have covered the land
nature's beauty go hand in hand
creating a magnificent postcard.
Snapshots of true volunteers
Notes of music rich and fluid
Surrounded by enchanting lullaby
Holds our ears in a sweet rock-a-bye
Red cardinals dressing the meadows
A symphony of exquisite hues
Show of amazing views
A rocking blast of wintery winds
Hold a chair
The miracle of winter wafting on the air
Stamped on hearts forevermore
Arrive at our door

Colorful Jewels

Toward evening end, the sun slowly turns
Into a crimson red
Drawn tender measuring upon a mead
A soft lavender and a blended
Swirling yellow exposure
Rich, (-) colors and pure
Colorful jewels sitting on the breast of the earth
Colors of burst umber, from the
Roaming herd at twilight
Waiting with anticipation of the night
Like an umbrella opening the darkness falls
All remains are charcoal
Silhouette scurrying for refuge in darkness

Tea Time

The time spent with my daughter
Still fills my mind with memories
Like morning sun, the gentle breeze
Quiet rustling of the trees
Dreams I could fly
This was a time, only to come to rest and be
A time for remembrance
When two lives with love glow in golden memories
A share of a cup of tea
A blessing to me
We can laugh, we can cry
Tell a story or two
"Mom and daughter," it's true!
Before long, the teapot was empty
Her cup and mine
How fast goes the time
Soon it's time to say goodbye
It's something before time will fly
My daughter and I share a cup of tea

Calling All Cooks

I learned about "calling all cooks,"
I wrote a book
Thanks to everyone devoted in endless hours
To handed down, from generation family favorites
The world's treasures to shared
Dedicated to my mother
Who taught me in a quiet morning
Sifting the flour
It has been a great experience for me
In this moment our hearts shared to be
Emotion of an experience long gone
A thought in memory never forgotten held on
It remains a world's treasured
Deep in the heart love measured

The World's So Big

The world's so big, how'll God find me?
He loves me
He knows every I'll be
I trust God last night.
I need to trust him today
Listen to my heart, not my head the devil can whisper
I'll trust God to walk in the right way
Fear is false evidence in appearing real
God's the only deal
Whenever a rainbow lights up the sky
God was very close all the way
Emotions seeping past hidden
Cracks in my heart
Migrated to that somewhere far apart

Girl with a Sewing Machine

She fastens with tiny stitches
Made a fine shirt
To go along the edge of formal skirt
Her face was written a wealth of happiness
Waiting for someone to wear with kindness
Ideas fly like musical notes played
Amazing ideas plan form
As thoughts are laid
A famous dressmaker, on the off chance
Her new plan has been advanced
She swept us from the sofa to hurry across the hall
She had to get busy before the fall
Deep inside another question pushed for an answer
The way things turned out
She left it to chance

The Behavior of Winter

Trees are arrayed in harvest of cold
Causing their leaves to look old
Winter preparing to dress
Them up so they can be put to bed
No sun, the weather was so
Unaccepting so darkness
Continued to spread
The night so clear look it had
Been hand drawn the moon
Casting brilliant silver cocoon
The night promised to be a frigid rain
Fueled by a deep chill
Winter has let to spill
The air had taken a definite sharpness to put place
A cold bitter night leaving in our space

About the Author

The author writes about places and people. They would write to fill the page with words of life-smart remarks, things they have experienced, and researched. They can't tell you the third step on the porch creaks. When roses are in bloom, the scent is everywhere. Writing's got to be real—feelings that conjured up dreams they were afraid to believe in. Know to start wherever you are.